the totality for kids

NEW CALIFORNIA POETRY

EDITED BY	ROBERT HASS
	CALVIN BEDIENT
	BRENDA HILLMAN
	FORREST GANDER

the totality for kids

JOSHUA CLOVER

UNIVERSITY OF CALIFORNIA PRESS   BERKELEY LOS ANGELES LONDON

University of California Press, one of the most distinguished
university presses in the United States, enriches lives around
the world by advancing scholarship in the humanities, social
sciences, and natural sciences. Its activities are supported by
the UC Press Foundation and by philanthropic contributions
from individuals and institutions. For more information, visit
www.ucpress.edu.

University of California Press
Berkeley and Los Angeles, California

University of California Press, Ltd.
London, England

Illustration for pages ii–iii: Constant Nieuwenhuys, *Gezicht
op New Babylonische sectoren* (View of New Babylon Sectors).
Collection of the Gemeentemuseum Den Haag. Photograph
© 2005 Artist Rights Society (ARS), New York/Beeldrecht,
Amsterdam.

Library of Congress Cataloging-in-Publication Data

Clover, Joshua.
    The totality for kids / Joshua Clover.
        p.   cm.—(New California poetry ; 16)
    Includes index.
    ISBN 0-520-24599-7 (alk. paper)—ISBN 0-520-24600-4 (pbk. :
alk. paper)
    I. Title.   II. Series.
PS3553.L667T68   2006
811'.54—dc22   2005021231

Manufactured in Canada

15   14   13   12   11   10   09   08   07   06
10   9   8   7   6   5   4   3   2   1

The paper used in this publication meets the minimum
requirements of ANSI/NISO Z39.48-1992 (R 1997) (*Permanence
of Paper*). ⊖

"Urbanism. Traffic," said Arturo with some chagrin. "Things on functional cities and reinforced concrete."

JULIO CORTÁZAR, FINAL EXAM

CONTENTS

the totality for kids

CERISERIE

Music: Sexual misery is wearing you out.

Music: Known as the Philosopher's Stair for the world-weariness which climbing it inspires. One gets nowhere with it.

Paris: St-Sulpice in shrouds.

Paris: You're falling into disrepair, Eiffel Tower this means you! Swathed in gold paint, Enguerrand Quarton whispering come with me under the shadow of this gold leaf.

Music: The unless of a certain series.

Mathematics: Everyone rolling dice and flinging Fibonacci, going to the opera, counting everything.

Fire: The number between four and five.

Gold leaf: Wedding dress of the verb *to have*, it reminds you of of.

Music: As the sleep of the just. We pass into it and out again without seeming to move. The false motion of the wave, "frei aber einsam."

Steve Evans: I saw your skull! It was between your thought and your face.

Melisse: How I saw her naked in Brooklyn but was not in Brooklyn at the time.

Art: That's the problem with art.

Paris: I was in Paris at the time! St-Sulpice in shrouds "like Katharine Hepburn."

Katharine Hepburn: Oh America! But then, writing from Paris in the thirties, it was to you Benjamin compared Adorno's wife. Ghost citizens of the century, sexual misery is wearing you out.

Misreading: You are entering the City of Praise, population two million three hundred thousand . . .

Hausmann's Paris: The daughter of Midas in the moment just after. The first silence of the century then the king weeping.

Music: As something to be inside of, as inside thinking one feels thought of,
   fly in the ointment of the mind!
Sign at Jardin des Plantes: GAMES ARE FORBIDDEN IN THE LABYRINTH.
Paris: Museum city, gold lettering the windows of the wedding-dress shops
   in the Jewish Quarter. "Nothing has been changed," sez Michael, "except
   for the removal of twenty-seven thousand Jews."
Paris 1968: The antimuseum museum.
The Institute for Temporary Design: Scaffolding, traffic jam, barricade, police
   car on fire, flies in the ointment of the city.
Gilles Ivain: In your tiny room behind the clock, your bent sleep, your Mythomania.
Gilles Ivain: Our hero, our Anti-Hausmann.
To say about Flemish painting: "Money-colored light."
Music: "Boys on the Radio."
Boys of the Marais: In your leather pants and sexual pose, arcaded shadows
   of the Place des Vosges.
Mathematics: And all that motion you supposed was drift, courtyard with
   the grotesque head of Apollinaire, Norma on the bridge, proved nothing
   but a triangle fixed by the museum and the opera and St-Sulpice in shrouds.
The Louvre: A couple necking in an alcove, in their brief bodies entwined
   near the Super-Radiance Hall visible as speech.
Speech: The bird that bursts from the mouth shall not return.
Pop song: We got your pretty girls they're talking on mobile phones la la la.
Enguerrand Quarton: In your dream gold leaf was the sun, salve on the
   kingdom of the visible.
Gold leaf: The mind makes itself a Midas, it cannot hold and not have.

Thus: I came to the city of possession.

Sleeping: Behind the clock, in the diagon, in your endless summer night, in the city remaking itself like a wave in which people live or are said to live, it comes down to the same thing, an exaggerated sense of things getting done.

Paris: The train station's a museum, opera in the place of the prison.

Later: The music lacquered with listen.

POEM

We always send it to the wrong address
And now that buoys even our most impersonal days. Everyone is beautiful!
And then almost everyone. *C'est cool-ça*, the shift that enchants the world
Or at least the afternoon of the world before it's off
To meet Chris and all at glimmering Colleen's
Arriving southside early and so twenty min for Lyn's *The Fatalist*
Amidst the superlit video store on the corner. It's funnier
In French: *superlit* but not much else. One is haunted
By the suspicion that one is in a society
Composed of people one will never meet for example
The Society That Thinks About Someone Named Anne-Lise
Occasionally. So I walk back around and up
The stairs and Chris puts on *either/or*. Elliott Smith 20th cen. American
Is nonetheless a star in the constellation
Our Romanticism and we have been hanging out
A lot there recently. A keener melancholy
About the music for a week or two afterward may be obvious
But something has to be done with the excess flowering inside death
Or is it just apotropaic? We'll see. The most awful thing
About the phrase "Every Germinal must have its Thermidor"
Is that one never gets to say so anymore
And really mean it. We lie down in categories
And wake up in concepts but must there be so much of the day spent

Tracking stray remarks and others' hearts
And maintaining a casual balance between OxyContin and "poetic prose"
So new sensations emerge? Meanwhile but I am happy
To see you! It's enough but not of anything.

EARLY STYLE

Ruins is utopia

From the perspective of

Before melancholy

And sex at the level of

Language promenading

Around the littoral of first

Failures of the codex

Colored morning

Pointing out over this

Being being being-left-empty

"ALAS, THAT IS THE NAME OF OUR TOWN; I HAVE BEEN CONCEALING IT ALL THIS TIME"

The stars were strange lightbulbs, the moon was half
A spectacle, they wandered into the vestibule
Of evening as the fat clouds fainted away,
Looking a little confused like one who arrives
Just a few minutes late for dinner to find flowers
Overgrowing the good silver, blossoms of baby yellow
And baby blue. Quel drag. Two boys climbed
Arm in arm toward the observatory, panting
And laughing on the long terraced steps. People ran
Up past the small balcony houses just to turn
And run down again, paying brief attention
To the many tastes of the balconistas, the hanging
Plants and decorations, that white facade ragged
With leftover wedding festoons. A woman
Walked backward up the stairs, leaving the library
To the rats and the readers (those modest mice),
And each person on the hill who noticed her
Daydreamy ascent recalled how much they enjoyed
Watching movies in reverse, the milk pouring upward
Into a blue-rimmed glass, into order, the undoing action
Of the sublime. Though barely evening it felt late
In the something, some larger shape which could not
Be seen though it pressed against you and seemed
To hum, a diversionary tune of so few notes

Repeated so indifferently it's hardly a tune at all,
Except what else could you call it? Who knows,
You answered, knowing most of the brilliant motion
To be already taken, the vast and whirling
Subterranean armature just now beginning
To wind down in earnest, and we have yet to invent
Anything so pure as the guillotine, an instrument
Known also as the little window. But what shall
We hope to see there? The marriage of the beautiful
And the trivial? That the sky finally
Emptied of clouds must now say a new thing?

BAROQUE PARABLE

The leopards eat the priests and slink from the temple in their robes.

New priests grow up through the paving stones in the plaza.

While we walked around in the pure systems summer guttered.

No one gets to heaven on the Rue Asymptote.

Our city like the collected gospels written on a single page.

Overgrown now with leopard-flowers and priest-flowers.

Can the alphabet be said to have its own weather?

Snow is falling in the margins of this story.

POEM

The brief capital of disturbances.
And within that city lies the city
Utopia with its little sojourns
And orange sodas, Utopia with
Its watermelons and televisions.
Inside, city that holds the happiest
Disturbances of my youth behind gold
Facades. Staggering up from the river
Full of forget in the flare of evening
One sees a city where the negative
Held its court. And inside that, city which
Is little more than a theory of red
In everyday life: red suburbs, rouge
Of nostalgia, series of scrawled changes.

UNDER THE PAVING STONES, THE BEACH

And so on, as one always arriving
Out of the faraway-far. The city
Where we rose slick into the rude rafters
Of the second story dazed after sex.
Inside that hangs the famed Somnopolis,
Purenight city leaking Seconal light.

Within is a blue unfinished city
Begun in dreamy cloudless gesture made
Dusty by the millions. City which is
A love letter. Interior to that,
City emerging naked from the white
Indifferences of winter. City
Once hidden in the library and now
Drowsing in the sleep of the collective.

BENEATH THE ABSTRACT LIVES THE EPHEMERAL

You cannot remember whether, at this
Corner, years before, you turned left or right.
Inside this immanent sigh, a city
Under the sign of the Ferris wheel,
The bullet-pocked clock tower. A city
Upflung from notes sprawled in the cool
Margins of the ghostly, the great cities.
City about nothing at all: it will not
Speak of me or others, of love or youth
Or anything else. And the city called
The Antipast toward which you travel
And travel, where rain is falling across
A grammar of skyline, rain is filling
The April air with silver quotation marks.

BLUE'S 1900

We belonged to the class with a gift for the theological niceties of things.

Often at night we had orchids in a light reduction of vinegar.

We wore necklaces of pale stones resembling scars.

And played at being the soldiers.

Who are gone into the transparency of the grave of the poem.

We lived in their work as you will live in ours.

We raised the Ferris wheel where they had garrisoned their horses.

And a calm leaked back into the deranged air above the world.

Blue must carry as much weight in this poem as in a painting or a suburb.

An index of being the hilarious.

Which has pursued us into this mystified minute.

THE OTHER ATELIER

Revolutionary workers remember the year

Contains dominated sectors like syntax and the city

So begins the Final Report on Words

Posted on handbills along the facades of Rue No Fun

The shift from modernism to world systems is stored in the new candy-colored currency

History and capital had been Astaire and Rogers but are now Clark Kent and Superman

Taking advantage of the exchange rate I have acquired a certain afternoon in 1953

Though it meant selling the rights to the word *peignoir*

And the neighborhood where you first heard it

Executive summary: Who is free on Sundays is anything but free

Sweetly and green two hundred winters

Are owed the Shah of Tomorrow

AEON FLUX: JUNE

Not sibylline but clear, empty weather; of the eight kinds of sky it was the
milk-paled potion most like a cup of coffee she poured past full in such a
way as to show herself how good she was, how the liquid lolled just over
the white cup's rim, just so the instant before an apology, until the surface
broke and color seeming singular though made of mix came sweetly over
the sides after which she could never think of herself as perfect again,
falling deeper into bright degradation as one falls down a well with great
relief, forgetting on the way how as a child she made her father stop at
every corner so she could sketch in her daybook the cross street and what
stores were where, using his back for a desk. But he never forgot, he felt the
markings each morning, a ghost tattoo about her he couldn't stop describing
to strangers: If there is writing in this place, he begins, it's only proof that
a tribe of pens once lived here, pardoning themselves in advance for their
mortal leap from a line of thinking to a half-lit field which starts under the
rubric of hay and fruit trees but seems to contain much more than mere
space allows, in the vicinity of sundown and all the nouns streaked with
gold, drowning in drachmas, lounging in louche, leading from the eye to
the distant mountain the guidebooks say is uninhabitable though behind
it squats a shack which is the summer home of God, finally free from
making cherries for the emperor's children; little God with his funny name
for which the other students teased him so, his elaborate notes.

AUTEUR THEORY

And then at the last second, after the conceptual, after graffiti, after the
Top 40, during architecture, after great pain, after mystery, after the feuilleton,
after the blue suburbs, after Malevich, after the rise of the South, after
indeterminacy, after Gerhard Richter, under the snow, after dinner, after
the red suburbs, after New French Girlfriend, after the movie, after unitary
urbanism, after indie rock,

ANTWERP RAINY ALL CHURCHES STILL HAUNTED

My name is Ferdinand the Word.

I have lived apart from the other words.

In the afternoon towns in the gray towns in June's fall.

Among the shadow-shaken riders of the yellow streetcars.

On their iron course past housing blocks and the rail terminal.

And the gothic panopticon of Cathedral Eleven.

The streetcar line a phrase which turns back wholly upon itself.

Being constructed letter by letter like a labyrinth.

Curtain of postwar reconstruction over the old town.

Electronica of the present humming behind the curtain.

To have a clerk call you comrade and dance off.

Across the air-white atrium amidst the experimental clothing.

Like she had seen into each pocket of you and found no money there.

It's like having a spike slipped from your forehead.

Which has been there since you were born.

You rise into the evening near the north steeple.

Amidst the seabirds and celesticons on their cloud-balcony.

Outside the work and peering down.

But you have come to sink into the book of the city.

Folded open to its moment.

Antwerp rainy all churches still haunted.

Each thing saying itself into the scribble and whisper.

Words on the yellow streetcars riding their one empirical sentence.

We turn round and round in the night and are consumed by fire.

OMA

A map is space in the form of rules, a map makes the beast with two spines.

Hell-beautiful the belle epoque boulevard is one axis and the other is twenty
Sentences welded in line, jointures smooth from use. We come to Images,
Images North, our turnoff is around here somewhere. Sometimes Morocco
Is Algeria. Beware ye th'electroglide downward to our constant New Babylon,
The City of the Captive Globe. Night comes to the name. Orpheus night,
Soi disant by les locals: smell of 20th cen. vomit, taste of dried flowers.

A-SHAPED GATE

With its A-shaped gate through which the west is consumed
Like water the city cannot be said to have a logic any more
Than the alphabet. All the citizens come from places
With emptying names, humping their boxes on their backs.
Some of bakelite or oiled bone and still others of marble—
The boxes make the form of the city and its deep design.
We have stacked them into walls, the walls into passageways
Spilling and folding to form palatial arcades, the arcades
Filled with a caustic ecstasy, a light more conducive to dreams
Than any drug, like the money-colored light of last century.
One hall is devoted to a choir of clocks, another to the engine
Used for affixing lovers to their beloveds, long since dismantled.
The city grows westward without any captain or brave music.
It makes other cities look like ponies wandering the plains.
If you live just outside the walls in the weird murmuring night,
You have been exiled from exile to memorize the murder ballads.

RUE DES BLANCS MANTEAUX

Certainly objects—places—writhe with uncertainty,
Not ours about them but their own. Promiscuous colors,
The summer truths. He was in love with yellow but unfaithful
With blue every chance he got. The sun kept the dayjail,
The nightjail had no keeper at all. His eyelids stuttered,
He wore his cell like a beautiful coat. His friends
Published a long list of his crimes in the paper ending
With Mythomania. The cops brought candy years later
To be remembered as a nature of things—a sweetness.

IN JAUFRÉ RUDEL'S SONG

The sun is abandoned into the thoughts one had about it.

The flowers lie fat on the field under the gong-filled air.

The field ends at the angry factor which keeps the numbers of the clock
   from flying off in twelve directions, beyond which his country.

She sends her voice into the pines, it returns at evening alone.

The crows hate her for her beauty, she is ugly as a poet.

There is a limited number of nights, though no particular night can
   prove this.

This is the greeting that the lovers exchange when they meet.

NO MORE BOFFINS

We were drinking gin and tonics on the terrace when the midi skirt
Came back into style. At this time movies were extremely popular
Although no more than usual, after which many people stopped in
At the Liberty Equality Fraternity Café for ice cream,
The ice cream of novel thoughts. Everyone was wearing
Those sunglasses everyone's wearing. Just a few felicities
Make a movement, the kind that should really have its own comic book
Exploring the great issues of the age but still with boffo action
And a speaking part for the lightbulb.
And so the crowd promenaded, lacking a manifesto,
Yet to have condemned the passéists or started the exclusions,
Scarcely aware they were (in the words of Archigram—
Clever boys, give them their own terrace immediately!)
A moment-village. They goeth abroad in the land.
How long have we been discussing whether we are a part
Of what passes by, and at what point did that become
The main conversation, replacing the summer, our cadastral survey
Of its many crowded quarters, its tuned suburbs and departments,
Its way of being a different sort of parade,
The kind which can be conveniently depicted with a spectrum?
Paint samples from Jane's Hardware will do in a pinch.
Already the fete is erasing itself from the popular memory
Like exploding instructions, leaving stained confetti as a reminder
You were supposed to get something done. Little tasks,
Large problems, philosophers say: Who will do the laundry

Now that history is coming to an end? What advantage
Would someone have over me who knew a direct route
From blue to yellow, far from this shady way station
Where we dream aimlessly of love in the afternoon,
The post-historical kind? However big you grow in my estimation,
You will always be a dwarf compared to these buildings,
Their skins glassy and inviting as that lake just to the west
Of wherever we grew up, you remember, Something Lake.
The information lurks in the shoals in forms by now
Almost unrecognizable. Now if only you could dive sideways.
When is the real holiday, the one for which everyone gets a sharp haircut,
Cruel atonal singing seeps from the crypt and the meaning of objects
Is once again up for grabs? Even bricks were once straw.

CHREIA

At this time there was an expectation of terror meaning cops in Kevlar and the green civic garbage cylinders sealed with discs of steel.

At this time the new train ran to an underground forest sheathed in books.

This time many years after the towers near the sex of the city were found to be twin cruets of jizz and sang.

We all floated with the same specific gravity in the constantly moving stream of money as of this time.

As in time of strike there was quite a bit of garbage loose in the street not like an Ourang-Outang in the Rue Morgue but it eddied and whorled at the edges of the seductively weeping stream.

I was riding a swan to the underground library or having sex with a swan under a shroud of words.

As of this time we kept a copy of the city in the library and another in the ether.

Constantly offered as a time of therefore but with a feeling of as.

Kevlar and carbines and garbage reduplicating into the quotidian in the time of the Plan Vigipirate.

Not more people in the street but more intensely as in the time of a transit strike promenading behind the veil of speech.

Around this time we thought of the skyline as new nature.

And through it flowed the invisible milk as through the ether and the sewers the milk of capital.

There was an expectation in everyday life.

It gathered in the dead spaces beside the endlessly grieving stream.

Of milk jizz and sang in the time of garbage in the vale of lang.

The shining order the burning simulations there are more of it.

LETTERS AND SODAS

There had been so much to talk about
As to set the rest in relief, beaming shyly after an era of being null.

Would it appear here, making its way
Unhurriedly through the museum barefoot? Or in a more tawdry form,
A huge face peering from the glass frontage
Of one of those new buildings? We are its blackbird.

It comes
To permeate our climate and indeed becomes it.
We meet ourselves more and more,
The frisson wears thin. Someone stayed in the room
With the lopsided bed and lunch left outside the door, the room
They had been given years before in another country.
Not a better one, though it had a lake.

But perfectly to scale. There were still rules of thumb
And untried combinations, Bunny and Blotto on the veranda
With atmosphere a and music m . . . sometimes we seemed to see
The edge of the construct but it was not our seeing
That counted, our songs under attic sun,
This rococo maquette of summer's end.

FRENCH NARRATIVES

A café. Nana wants to leave Paul. The pin-table.
The record shop. Two thousand francs. Nana lives her life.
The concierge. Paul. The Passion of Joan of Arc. A journalist.
The police. Nana is questioned.
The boulevards. The first man. The room.
Meeting Yvette. A café in the suburbs. Raoul. Gunshots in the street.
The letter. Raoul again. The Champs-Élysées.
Afternoon. Money. Washbasins. Pleasure. Hotels.
A young man. Luigi. Nana wonders whether she's happy.
The streets. A bloke. Happiness is no fun.
Place du Châtelet. A stranger. Nana the unwitting philosopher.
The young man again. The oval portrait. Raoul trades Nana.

ÇA IRA

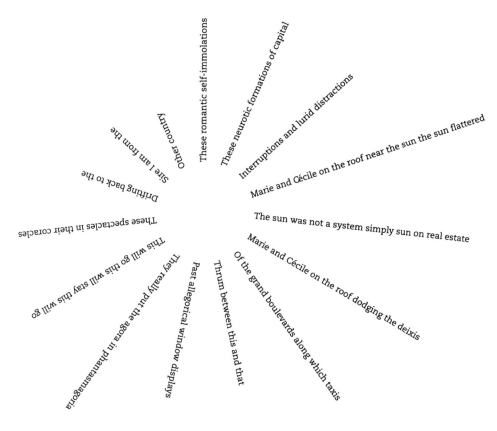

These romantic self-immolations

These neurotic formations of capital

Interruptions and lurid distractions

Marie and Cécile on the roof near the sun the sun flattered

The sun was not a system simply sun on real estate

Marie and Cécile on the roof dodging the deixis

Of the grand boulevards along which taxis

Thrum between this and that

Past allegorical window displays

They really put the agora in phantasmagoria

This will go this will stay this will go

These spectacles in their coracles

Drifting back to the

Site I am from the

Other country

KANTINE

And then at the last second, after Malevich, after Gerhard Richter, after
the conceptual, after graffiti, after the feuilleton, after indeterminacy, after
New French Girlfriend, after indie rock, after the Top 40, after great pain,
after dinner, after the movie, after mystery, after unitary urbanism, after
the blue suburbs, after the red suburbs, after the Rise of the South, during
architecture, under the snow,

POEM

We are bored in the city, there is no longer any temple of the sun!
How many times have you walked at evening, Taxi Street to Rue No Fun,
Past the post office steps where lovers sprawled like sensual corpses intend us
To see Zone as one lost, city of haphazard marvels and haciendas?
Ahh, they are dreaming of dreaming, as poems do. They are made of poppies,
As all lovers have been shown to be; they are made of paper, like philosophy.
Here's an example: "Words are the shadows thrown by ideas, pure surface—
Nothing affixes them to the page but their indolent desire to be seen twice,
Otherwise they would lift from the sheaves of lonely monks and the languors
Of lonely wives, umber wings blurring into evening's blur." The danger
Of philosophy is that the mayor is weeping over *Love Will Tear Us Apart*
(The last chapter where Aglaya gets it) in his disheveled terrace apartment
And having a better time. And look! Here are Aglaya and the lovelorned
Chtcheglov, next-to-last chapter, their eyes black poppies in the lunar
Gloom of the post office steps. They have seen you once before,
Dancing to tiny music on the newly invented Street of Piano Tuners.

THE DARK AGES

Many people had candles and torches were a dime a dozen. "You Light
Up My Life" was one of the most popular songs. What about illuminated
manuscripts, and those lightbulbs every time they had an idea—imagine
how that must have been in the Dark Ages! Stealth would favor the village
idiot, but a wise man would be as a strobe light in a rainstorm. Once in the
Dark Ages, believing the precinct to be deserted, I wandered as one lost. Then
the beams of a passing car would light the street for some distance, all the
other faces flashing *here, here, here* like terrible saints. A woman with metal
teeth. Two boys in a doorway tending another's wounds. I was looking for
you. Think how useful saints must have been, roman candles of the Dark
Ages, you could prop them in a hayloft and serve drinks. But almost always
when we talk about light we mean it in some theoretical way, as in the word
"deluxe." In poetry the line is something like a lamp-lit way onto which you
have just turned, nodding lilies and a couple of desperadoes under the eaves.
The line break we would call darkness, for there the street ends, the lamp
fails, and all is occluded. In the near distance someone has chalked *chicas
serpientes,* pale blue on a clay wall and now this is part of the line too, it must
now include snakes. Halfway down the street a spot between the near and
far lamps is almost dark though things are visible beyond it. Something
could be happening there, breathless, obscure, two voices. Most of the poems
from the Dark Ages are very short, about a neighborhood in size. But then
there are the epics, always about travel and in the form of a thousand
neighborhoods stitched together, each one with its little snakes and obscure
lovers, or other things altogether, a low balcony in which someone has
placed flowers carved from wood even in this district where fresh flowers

are in long supply. An old woman carries a bale of lilies down the street, each a white burn on a green fuse. Suppose you are waiting for me at the end of each line; I mean, you said you were in that letter from the Dark Ages. Past the little snakes and the little criminals, past the little flowers, a girl sitting on a low wall with a boy between her knees. The faces *here, here,* the blue chalk glowing like neon. And now I have come to some town square and the strangers look at me as if I had done something terrible, an otherwise good man who commits murder after murder to understand why exactly he did it the first time.

EN ABYME

Here in the duskgarden it's getting so you can't tell
an abyss from a pageant. We think of stars as brief words

which blink on at evening saying something we would like
to say also. Words are flowing toward mysterious black coasts.

One passes near the kind of village usually found in the Japan
of pictures. And it is a picturesque village

don't you think? I loved it and hope to visit it some day.
It was there you fell into exile among *the laughing children*

of the laughing class. Now we are older and empty
into the winedark sentence the inkdark sea.

"AN ARCHIVE OF CONFESSIONS, A GENEALOGY OF CONFESSIONS"

Now the summer air exerts its syrupy drag on the half-dark
City under the strict surveillance of quotation marks.

The citizens with their cockades and free will drift off
From the magnet of work to the terrible magnet of love.

In the far suburbs crenellated of Cartesian yards and gin
The tribe of mothers calls the tribe of children in

Across the bluing evening. It's the hour things get
To be excellently pointless, like describing the alphabet.

Yikes. It's fine to be here with you watching the great events
Without taking part, clinking our ice as they advance

Yet remain distant. Like the baker always about to understand
Idly sweeping up that he is the recurrence of Napoleon

In a baker's life, always interrupted by the familiar notes
Of a childish song, "no more sleepy dreaming," we float

Casually on the surface of the day, staring at the bottom,
Jotting in our daybooks, how beautiful, the armies of autumn.

"OF THE CITY OF THE DARK . . ."

The desire to have been inside it will one day set us in motion
Elsewhere—the ever-nearer. Was this the fizzy presabsence
So famous one summer between steam and the panoramas?

Somehow we became friends with the mayors and managers
Of the necropolis of symbols once seen only at a distance
Across water. He lived there on intimate terms with an iguana.

Something can no longer be read in the latest billboards
And the facades along the canal have been sheathed in mirrors.
The neighborhood which is a continent and every room a cathedral

Must be every neighborhood. A certain amount of monumentality
With one's coffee will not overturn the hay cart of everyday life
And must be abandoned yet again if we would like to be captive

To experimental forms of the game. We the delandscaped.
We who have showed fine and lyrical deference toward any of this.
All this drawing near. All these boat-shaped cities Louis-Georges

All these railings made of iron sentences ending. All these
New guidebooks with their colors indexed to tell us how to feel
When we get there. All this time with its greener-than-thou.

POEM

Tired of people, I wanted the mail to come
Announcing tiny changes, still sufficient.
I felt stuck in an early passage as the others
Floated ahead on rootless islands with mastlike palms
To which they clung as the false wind of flying
Into the next part blew their hair and clothes out
Behind them. This would have been comical
Had I not been left near the beginning hence
Having little or no idea of what was going on
Compared to them. They have made it as far
As Connecticut, a confab with something
On the rocks amidst the overtures of the obscure
Neighbors. Out the window one can see
A figure in a black cape signifying bad luck.
He's been bad so long he thinks he's human.
"So don't we all, John, so don't we all." Clink.
They barely remember the beginning, filled
With hopeful flirtations and just strolling around
As it was, an ascending afternoon of what seemed
At the time like pure space before the way things
Ought to move forward reared its ugly head.
The story took on aspects other than April,
The docks filled and emptied, strangers waved
Into distance. All that to-ing and fro-ing
Would later be seen as a single motion,

More or less what the stars are up to,
Wearing grooves in their surface. Now Christ,
Even the creeps come wiser than I—where is my
Autumn, where my lacklustrine kingdom?

VALIANT EN ABYME

Our grand peregrinations through these temporary cities,
These pale window box poppies of the laughing class,
Drifting as if time came in the same long dollops as starlight,
Resemble an epic journey as a coffee bean resembles a llama's foot,
Though the kitchen table may be far from the desert
It's near in spirit, a yellow oasis before the wind
Starts its restless sweeping of white flower-dust across the lintel,
Marking the fine edge of things like children asleep
At the opera, piled up near the door, summer passing
On its way out. Prince Valiant vowed to sew the horizons
Into a single idea, to put on the blue dress of distance,
Looping past rivers and mountains as one leaps from bed
To bed to make loneliness lonely, the suburbs were for him
A relief, a pageant of calm desire where he settled,
All the king's horses grazing on forsythia out back
While the evening tilts back out of the night, a kindly drunk
Uncle, and asks you to stay. Was this the end of traveling?
Or just a change in the story over time, as for example how
Tous les chevaux du roi become Josie and the Pussycats
From one version to the next? So all heroes are deranged
By something quite common yet unexpected, a constellation
Redrawn and named again though the stars
Above the porch don't shift but seem to sink
Through winter's pitcher of noircotic ink,

Leaving a single streetlight that burned happily,
Thinking it was the sun, after all it was the day
Of the night and turned the world around it,
We were good sentences and forgot where we started.

FERAL FLOATS THE FORM IN HEAVEN AND OF LIGHT

The famous and the dead have learned to fall between our eyes
And their forms in heaven: a philosophical eclipse
Which edges them in light, like bodies in the nineteenth-century
Photo plates enwrapped in their emanations and pale shrouds.
They have their own cities called Necropolis and New York
Built of what they are said to have said, the famous and the dead.
In your gleaming imitations where the density of things
Howls through the evening's blue precincts you hurry home
To practice passing drinks from mouth to mouth, you the mere,
The living, lit only by a faint electricity whose mind is elsewhere.
You wrote of them often, kissed one once, there is a picture
Of you in your chair at the end of the century, thinking their cities
Until an aura and awfulness surrounded you, a motion appearing
As no motion at all, the inverse of a wave, a demonology—

PARABLE LESTRANGE

Sign says one is always approaching the river.

Through the metropolis through duration.

Past the windows of the wine merchant the bookseller the butcher.

And each has smeared with bars of soap pale prices there.

C went with his very being toward language.

Later this was discovered to be a way-things-are.

A motion without a mate in which we all paraded.

Lonely soldiers.

Behind the long spinning water a windowless room.

Here at zero his name zeroes.

Things and the ghost-characters of things in sexual embrace.

The odalisque asleep by the inkwell.

POEM

So I went out into the nervous system of the air—

Bearing beneath my lettrist overcoat my village
The monumental city long ago breathed in
And held
       Went out into the signal and static—
Rivermutter steeplebell and traffic—net of noise
Knotted by sirens
                Into the brutal red dream
Of the collective—humming there behind the parade
Of the ideal citizen—in which I took my place

Saint of the negative in my velvet suit

My howlings pressing outward against the million
Other howlings—the deformed din of the I-AM

So you see the net drawing close—the false escape
Of recollection
            How my unhausmannized town

Within a town was myth below the shadows of the new
Towers reaching after the breathlimit—

And there was no way not to be during—architecture

And violence are the natural language of *crowds*—

APORIA

Peoria! With your unshaven boys
Smooching on the street corners or talking
On the phone while skating headlong into
Tourists who throng the ghosty avenues
Of Peoria! With your grand soirees
And jubilations pushing out against
The weight of history—Peoria
"Capital of the nineteenth century"!
With your cloud of excess signs and gold leaf
Settling on the eyelids of black-haired
Women glowing from the terrace cafés
Which line the stone banks of Kickapoo Creek
Flowing like blue milk under the bridges
Of Peoria! And your swank manners
And red suburbs and no future and movies
Where strangers swap philosophical gems
And fall at once into bed—never have
So few of all possible kisses
Involved me as in Peoria
Midwestern city o' lights! And so off to
Glamorous Vernon city of canals
Five-step bridges with arcane graffiti
With its three million atavistic
Pigeons at the heart of a jewel-box
Labyrinth and its ancient library

Drooping languorously into the lagoon
A few inches per annum bearing Tom Swift
Down to the Doges. Vernon with its dead
Ends and no vistas and supermodels
In their sunglasses and autumn exile
Like the four figures in "The Mystical
Marriage of Saint Catherine" (attrib.
Parmigianino) seemingly torn
From a glossy and glued to the abyss:

Everywhere at once I must be with you!

A BOY'S OWN STORY

And then at the last second, after the Top 40, under the snow, after the conceptual, after the blue suburbs, after great pain, after the feuilleton, after graffiti, after the Rise of the South, after the movie, after unitary urbanism, during architecture, after mystery, after Gerhard Richter, after indeterminacy, after indie rock, after Malevich, after the red suburbs, after dinner, after New French Girlfriend,

RETURN TO RUE DES BLANCS MANTEAUX

When we arrived it was much as we expected, we had
Sent our imaginings ahead to do the dirty work: a small arch
On a street of windows gang'd with ghostly wedding gowns
Opening onto a sudden place which wanted us—all this
In the late afternoon beneath the balcony of having to return.

WHITEREAD WALK

Vertigo Europa austere museum sex hotel record shop Odeon neon breath
isolations in the vale of lang climbing the Whispering Gallery doing the
Strand glad girls paper wedding painted retina crosses a small continent
between two bars colored rays of visible things in the Spring in the
superlative Hotel Europa Drag the light of the past tense falls from an
iron hotel railing a long skirt drenched in lassitude all Polaroids are out
of focus felt anagogic the taxi came thwack we drove into a book

THEIR AMBIGUITY

Against things made things, new desires. But I had wanted to tell you about

my town and already we have reached the problem of the new. Absurdity is
Are you for or against Brigitte Bardot,the Rolling

the new beauty. Ugly is the new black. Three is the new closure. This is
Stones, small cars, hippies, nationalization, spaghetti, old people, the United Nations, mini-

the story of the new noun, set in relation to what it must replace—everything
skirts, pop art, thermonuclear war, hitch-hiking?   *Each word, idea, or*

that becomes equipage for lifestyles. But no, the relations are the new nouns,
symbol is a double agent. Some words, like "fatherland" or the policeman's uniform, usually

and they will sing our forms back to us, almost unrecognizably. It's a new
work for authority; but make no mistake, when ideologies clash or simply begin to wear out,

town, natch.
the most mercenary sign can become a good anarchist.

New every day! Adrift in Late Contingency, addicted to symbols, to paper,

addicted to our roles, tangled in the worn grid of the city the new city is still trying to swear off. Smeared ink, you're soaking in it. It's a little like having

The spectacle's time: time for a kiss,

two memories at once. Then you realized there would be a series of these

snapshot time.

things, a composite view called the flower of individualism. Now an electronic

texture is the only one that can deal with sentiment, memory, and imagination,

a whirlpool in which objects can regard themselves without tragedy. It is, as

Whatever you possess possesses you in return.

they say, très contemplatif—the latest style.

When a poem by Mallarmé

becomes the sole explanation for an act of revolt, then poetry and revolution will have overcome

The very mention of which summons up our beloved revolutionary sweetheart

their ambiguity.

with his cup of days, his notes on the brooch, the Ravachol, the hemline. The

That's why I prefer you to wear to this party,

sweet disposition of his blow-stuff-up-ism. To be a client of chance where

since it is out of season, and just official and administrative, some marvelously crafted artificial

client is the only role available, a tiny ideology unfolding until outsideless. If

flowers.

one attunes one's feelings to the perspective of the clock, dismal spires will
I have had

give onto the new noun, implied in language's need to make more language.
quite enough of calling Ruins those facades that for three years now have displayed their fire-

But from the map's point of view, downtown must arrive eventually at the
blackened statues, visited by the moon and young ladies from whose Tyrolean hats white veils

ambience of the inverted neighborhood: as streets lead to rueful erotic
flutter—the coquetry of a metropolis brazenly new, rich, and splendid.

dreaming, boulevards lead to suburbs. In the suburbs of Paris now they pray

to Allah and the smoke is sweet. In America the new suburb is the endgame

of SuperStudio, the megastructure realized as a social form.

Agreement held us captive: down quantity street, everything is of a muchness.

This is an idea, this is a box of Orange Jell-O. The debate over whether one is

an architect or a construction worker, the slow war between artists and ouvriers,
Nature exists, and cannot be added to; apart from cities, railway lines, and several

is kept on the downlow so as not to interfere with our long season of the
inventions of our making.

ineffable, lined with a profound feeling to which shreds of melancholy still

cling. I have nothing and must have everything. And so we wave good-bye

to the happiest disorders of youth; après ça, la mystification. Isn't this getting

rather, well, French? The Disney version, smash le system. Still, a year inside
Thus revolutions and counterrevolutions

the glitches is an education for a busy child, desperate vertigo between two
follow hard upon one another's heels, sometimes within a twenty-four-hour period—in the

moments, intensity without departure.
space, even, of the least eventful of days.

But deep down inside, every mercenary dreams of killing the king.

That absence of an intensely desired presence, how quickly it moves from

invention to basic banality, and yet for now it makes looking good again,
An empty space creates

immersive, as when you first guessed you were in it, and not just its creature.
a full-filled time.

Over the slate roofs, there was a framework on which to hang the appearances,

though just ignoring it seems more fun. To speak of when we were modern

is to invoke a drowsy and forgetful god. And look! There are the cranes and
This project could be compared

yellow helmets of the workers hoisting the new noun into the hacienda of
with the Chinese and Japanese gardens of illusory perspectives — with the difference that those

the air, amidst some trees and red arrows, in the last evenings of summer.
gardens are not designed to be lived in all the time.

The content of the town is our pleasure; everything that remains is form,

though one could say the same thing about the totality for kids.

WHITEREAD WALK

Monumental the lacunae between illbiquitous promenaders down to the Square past the Open 24 Hours as social forms of grieving we are prohibited this is the remix the new glitch has been recalled melancholy of luscious Pictober the fall of the phenomenon into the iris back with another one of those Return of the Flaneur as hardcore Autumnophage echolocation always places you in a different country the cure is beats per minute bad year in Brooklyn Bombs Over Baghdad the negative needs no introduction and/or here we go!

FOR THE LITTLE SOLDIER

So it turns out I am totally a Knight Templar at loose ends now that the Crusades are discredited and the banking industry is controlled by lawyers which like New Yorkers is really just code for Jews. Now I like to read magazines called things like *TeleStar* and *Shock* and post to my blog in what *Teen People* called the latest in mediated indifference. Sometimes I like to compose little poems and imagine you reading them. I like to pretend you are a real person dressed in a suit selling copies of Mao's Little Red Book on Sproul Plaza and declaiming your favorite passages at lunchtime. You do not know a town until you know where the drunkards go to piss. Until you know the daydreams occupying the woman on the assembly line you do not know the country. Of course there are many systems to put those dreams there inside her amphitheatrical skull operated by people known as affect workers like you and me and Drew Barrymore. We help people feel certain ways and are paid a living wage plus the little bit extra called the hook or the sting—a small but pleasant feeling like a tiny holographic version of meeting the president. The imagination resembles nothing so much as a salon for special expositions in a museum closed because it's the First of May. In this way it can be distinguished from politics—history's coliseum where the great powers set the lesser at each other's throats.

LATE STYLE

A dark shadow of friendship began to appear.
It is beautiful because most music
Is not very good.
Feeling that we live is itself pleasant
Though it does not bring you any closer.

X continued to equal X
But as a sort of courtesy.
It got to be later in the day.
There was a certain innocence nonetheless;
A new system had been installed.

But the great reminiscences, the historical shudder—.

A part of it will never be occupied
Though the weather of the times will always rain
On its abstraction and we will feel a great affinity
With the buildings scrawled there.

YEAR ZERO

The clock into which you stared as into a mother's face now seen as a time-factory under winter.

Year Zero the mistakes have yet to be invented and music—well it comes down to inventing flowers.

This they do down at the flower factory over the bridge from the factory where cherries tumble from the cherry-making machinery.

Nothing is true everything is the case.

Paused at the edge of the tub turning away wanting to be seen.

Morning apartment where the light has lost its yellow at the moment of the sign.

Turns away wants to be seen.

Just then you turned to look—a sweetness with a hook on either end.

Surely it is the century of clouds?

A long walk across town with your social realist overcoat turned up: citizens yawning on the passing train.

The train windows blurring past like movie frames run sideways starring our exhausted revolutionary sweetheart whose head cracks open to swallow the day.

We have made the world flat once again.

Meetings in the cold warehouse on the outskirts of the Year Zero.

In the red suburbs of the Year Zero.

In the other night on the other side of permission you could have her or a police car on fire if you preferred the second you wore a black square on your jacket or in your hair.

The machine flower the machine music blotted out all other sounds still you could not get it loud enough.

Needs to know looks back.

Wants to be seen turns away.

Had meant to write the century of crowds.

And beneath it the gear rooms of the calendar where tiny cracks have been discovered in every hour time has started to trickle staunched with grease and sweat a shudder a sadness at waking.

Now must begin again it must be new time.

In the morning of the sign lying in bed in cold Utopia and alone under the black square.

Your ears swelled with flowers a corpse in your mouth.

You are free though a freedom with its ribs showing.

QU'Y-A-T-IL D'AMÉRICAIN DANS LA POÉSIE AMÉRICAINE?

Au fond c'est fait en sable.
Heureusement, parce que sans ça, c'était un véritable casse-tête.
Bienvenue au désert du réel,
Je suis un éphémère et point trop mécontent citoyen.
Je ne crois pas que la révolution soit finie.
J'ai donc habité, pendant ces années, un pays où j'étais peu connu,
Avec la foudre des dieux qui protège la toundra islandaise de la publicité,
De grands dieux rouges, de grands dieux jaunes, de grands dieux verts,
fichés sur le bord des pistes spéculatives que l'esprit emprunte d'unsentiment à
    l'autre, d'une idée à sa conséquence
En passant devant les fiers immeubles gras comme un gros sac d'argent. Je
    souhaiterais pouvoir demeurer dans cette ville agréable et conventionnelle,
Cette forme tranquille, cette forme modeste, mais qui prétend au plaisir,
Puis s'évanouit dans les brouillards d'un hypnoLondres.
Tous sont à la bonne place dans ces galeries aux réverbérations optiques,
Les chevaux des cieux aux ailes de cygnes, dont la crinière agite la musique de l'été,
Le brave Dingbat de Los Angeles,
Une femme au foyer de n'importe quel quartier de n'importe quelle ville de n'importe
    quel coin du Mexique un samedi soir.
Chaque dimanche est trop peu de dimanche,
Un tombeau vivant, le véritable tombeau du crâne.
Qu'en un glatz lev'e jatz desiratz.
Fo trobatz en durmen sus un chivau
Je me promène. Principalement, je me promène.

WHAT'S AMERICAN ABOUT AMERICAN POETRY?

They basically grow it out of sand.
This is a big help because otherwise it was getting pretty enigmatic.
Welcome to the desert of the real,
I am an ephemeral and not too discontented citizen.
I do not think the revolution is finished.
So during these years, I lived in a country where I was little known,
With the thunder of the Gods that protect the Icelandic tundra from advertising,
Great red gods, great yellow gods, great green gods, planted at the edges of the
    speculative tracks along which the mind speeds from one feeling to another,
    from one idea to its consequence
Past the proud apartment houses, fat as a fat money bag. I wish that I might
    stay in this pleasant, conventional city,
A placid form, a modest form, but one with a claim to pleasure,
And then vanish in the fogs of a hypnoLondon.
All are in their proper place in these optical whispering-galleries,
The swan-winged horses of the skies with summer's music in their manes,
The basic Los Angeles Dingbat,
A housewife in any neighborhood in any city in any part of Mexico on a
    Saturday night.
Every Sunday is too little Sunday,
A living grave, the true grave of the head.
In one shout desire rises and dies.
Composed while I was asleep on horseback
I drift, mainly I drift.

AT THE ATELIER TELEOLOGY

The sun tutoyers me! Adrift beyond heroic realism
In the postmodern sublime where every window can lie
Like a priest, adrift in the utopia for bourgeois kittens
Having of late learned the trick of how to listen to two
Songs at once—double your measure double your fun!—
It seems to defy death and still the commodity
Is not cast down. I say Frank O'Hara was an anarchist,
Nothing else explains all that joy. Exclamation point!
He was not a systems guy. At the end of Beckett's version
Of "Zone" the new century rips the head off the old
And calls it the sun and that's joy too, the anarchic sun
Leaping out of a fin de siècle type of sparagmos
So it can make with the rendezvous a century later
And greet me all casual as if we were old friends,
Where did you get those shoes, how's Rodefer doing,
Who's sleeping in their warehouse studio and oh
By the way Joshua why are you so obsessed with the modern
And its endnotes, what about going to bed in the sensuous
Now and Here, you know, the *sublime* sublime? These are all
Good questions, which explains how you got to be the sun,
And I know it's not an easy job, knowing everything
Half the time or half of things all the time, melting
Everybody's cacao whisky, being called names by poets,
And other tasks and tribulations, this world,
This half-read hebdomaire, this jacquerie of knickknacks.

All in day's work, sun sez, adopting a comical Bolshevik
Accent, but please, tell those boys to stop writing poems
For Lili Brik, it doesn't get more homosocial than that.
So I am wondering if the sun is the last soviet, the self-
Sustaining factory of the sun, but just as I begin to wonder
Into the old haunts under the scarlet letter H, the cold
Afternoons of Vitebsk and the Dziga Vertov, Dziga Vertov,
I recall my new friend and shout over my shoulder
Thanks for the advice! Anytime, after all, it's free,
Say hello to the generation that burned itself in effigy.

It turns out everything is the world in miniature and this was not good news

In the magazine racks in the downtowns in the video arcades while the band
danced in a café in two suits and a dress

I turned twenty-one in parole doing prison without life

It is a beautiful night we live in the world

Of the antilyric and the train that bears money into the city

Where it is at its happy-go-luckiest after a season socked

Away in the cabinet of a country house bordered on all sides by the austere cinematic light of mid-century

When the money arrived it leapt the canals gracefully sometimes in the skins of men

And sometimes leaping more abstractly through the city

Between bare consciousness and the bourse of basic beliefs

Where as the pocket philosophes often say "everything is connected"

An idea that casts the Janus-shadows of paranoia and mysticism and still is not mistaken

We could not understand until we had been there in the long hallways in the passages in the upstairs windows low under the glass roofs

We survive in the speech of what voices

We the alphabet present in a purely spoken language

Ah America you have got worn thin
Plus unable to hold Americans

In the morning citizens loiter on the little bridge beneath the latest billboards
Talking on mobile phones in popular modern languages and the jargon
   of birds

All the Futurists are in the past giving the sense history
Really has ended sometime around El Lissitzky

In the evening one is always coming upon some square
Where meaning has already congealed amidst architecture students
   and beer

You love one of them from a shy distance
As melancholy Albania loves indifferent France

It seems important to have a theory of
Writing based on Giorgio the painter de Chirico

Lest a leisurely debate on dreams brawl into the street
And occupy our attentions until it's time to sleep

There is no pleasure like wasting time in your city divided into quarters
   sisters and zones
Beneath the clattering gears of the moon and the sun

Oh most industrial and beguiling of lullabies
Heard at the wedding of Sonia Terk and Robert Delaunay

It is a beautiful night we live in the world
Of the antilyric that is still sung in the city's dominated sectors

The Blue Bar is closing and the Orange Bar is closed
I wonder how friends are while walking home

Sleeping and dreaming are dialectical dear
I have a fragment in my head Apollinaire

You go to the black suburb, *Et in arcadia ego*. Past Arrival Street, you is
ambiguous. Many things are music of which some *[six or seven words struck
out and illegible]* for me as he was to almost all the younger ones, a stranger,
Et in arcadia ego. The art of the present comes down to four discrepant
images of B. B. turning toward us, toward our shared machine eye, our deep
disfluency. Out past Arrival Street we go to the black suburb, we are buried in
Grant's Tomb, *Et in arcadia ego*, we walk in the garden of his turbulence, *Et in
arcadia ego*, we are in a station of the metro, we are lost in the editing of July,
we too lived in arcades in arcades you will find us.

ACKNOWLEDGMENTS

The author would like to thank the following people, in addition to Laura Cerruti, my editor at the University of California Press: Seeta Chaganti, Jeff Clark, T. J. Clark, Carol Clover, Marie De Gandt, Gudrun Ensslin, Steve Evans, Andrew Joron, Courtney Love, Jennifer Moxley, Geoffrey G. O'Brien, Jennifer Scappettone, and Stephen Smith. "Poem (We always send it to the wrong address)" is for Chris Nealon. "The Other Atelier" is for Ange Mlinko. "At the Atelier Teleology" is for Charles Altieri. This book is dedicated to Louis-Georges Schwartz: *When I sing, I do not sing for me, but I sing for a friend who is close to me* (Prince Gaston Phébus).

Poems from this volume appeared previously (sometimes in somewhat different form) in the following places: *The Addison Street Anthology, American Poetry Review, The Baffler, Bay Area Poetics, Best American Poetry* (2001, 2003), *Black Warrior Review, The Boston Review, The Canary, Five Fingers Review, The Hat, Interim, Jacket, Near South, The New Young American Poets, Ploughshares, Sycamore Review,* and *Volt.* "Whiteread Walk" (both) and "Their Ambiguity" appeared in the chapbook *Their Ambiguity* (Quemadura, 2003).

INDEX

Rogers, Ginger, 15
Rolling Stones, 51
Romanticism, 6, 30
Roussel, Raymond, 10
Ruins, 8, 53

Saint Paul's Cathedral in London, 50
Saint-Sulpice church in Paris, 3, 4
Schwartz, Louis-Georges, 37
Seconal, 12
Sex: of the city, 26; and dazedness, 12; and
    melancholy, 8; and misery, 3; with swan,
    26; between things, 43
Shakespeare, William, 20
Simmel, George, 26
Situationists. See Bernstein, Michèle;
    Chtcheglov, Ivan; Debord, Guy;
    Vaneigem, Raoul
Situationist slogans, 4, 12
Sleep, 3, 4, 5, 13, 40, 64, 67, 68
Somnopolis, 12
Spring, 6, 50
Stevens, Wallace, 15
Stone Temple Pilots, 32
Streetcars, 18, 19
Street names: Arrival Street, 68; Rue
    Asymptote, 11; Rue Morgue, 26; Rue
    No Fun, 15, 32; Street of Piano Tuners,
    32; Taxi Street, 32
Sublime, the, 9, 64

Suburbs: black, 68; blue, 14, 17, 31, 48;
    cinematic, 29; far, 36; Parisian con-
    trasted with American, 53; red, 12,
    17, 31, 46, 48, 60; tuned, 24; visited
    by Prince Valiant, 40
Summer, 5, 11, 22, 28, 36, 37, 40, 55, 62, 63
Sun: abandonment of, 23; antisystematic,
    30; clattering gears of, 67; dayjail kept
    by, 22; dream of, 4; friendly conversa-
    tion with, 64–65; streetlight as noctur-
    nal, 41; temple of, 32
Superman, 15
Sweethearts, revolutionary, 52, 60
Swift, Tom, 47

Tears for Fears, 36
Terk, Sonia, 68
Thermidor, 6
Tininess, 4, 32, 38, 52. See also
    Monumentality
Towers, 13, 19, 26
Trains, 5, 18, 26, 54, 60, 65

Ugliness, 23, 51
University of California at Berkeley, 57
Urbanism, 17, 31, 48
Utopia, 8, 12, 61, 64

Vale of lang, 27, 50
Valiant, Prince, 40

DESIGNER
Jessica Grunwald

TEXT
8.25/13 Caecilia Roman

DISPLAY
Gotham

INDEXERS
Andrew Joron and Joshua Clover

COMPOSITOR
BookMatters

PRINTER AND BINDER
Friesens Corporation